D0549814

Watching the Lights Go Out

This is the first-person non-fiction account of several years in the lives of a man approaching retirement and his chocolate Lab as she gradually loses her sight. It painstakingly traces the subtle but inexorable changes in Bessie, an exuberant passionate retriever and lover of humanity, as she struggles to make sense of a world of increasing darkness and learns to compensate for her disability. As Bessie adapts, so does he; his behaviors alter in response to her behaviors. He becomes more watchful, mindful, compassionate, and also ingenious as he dreams up ways to make her life easier and better. His love for her grows and grows.

While Bessie's condition was supposed to progress from diagnosis to total blindness in a year, she manages, miraculously, to hold on to some of her sight for two and a half years. During this long period, she refuses to allow what is happening to her to slow her down, to change her routines, or to modify the things she loves to do.

Though the narrator's retirement after over forty-two years of teaching and school administration is referred to only a few times, it seems to me it's really the subtext of the book; he sees (or fears) parallels between what is happening to Bessie and what will happen to him, psychologically or physically. Perhaps the borders of his life will close in; perhaps he will no longer be able to do the things he loves; perhaps his routine will change irrevocably; perhaps with advancing age he will become more dependent, less capable.

Happily that doesn't happen for him any more than it does for Bessie, and the lessons that he takes from the resolution, courage, and unconscious dignity of his dog he shares with the reader.

Steven Bauer, author of several well-known books including The Strange and Wonderful Story of Robert McDoodle (The Boy Who Wanted To Be a Dog). **Simon & Schuster**

BESSIE'S STORY

Watching
the Lights Go Out

**A devoted dog's advancing blindness
provides timeless life-lessons on the art of
aging gracefully**

*To Jim — Be Strong
and spread joy!*

THOMAS W. FARMEN

Printed in the United States of America

First Printing, 2018

ISBN 978-1-7326470-0-8 (paperback, black & white)
ISBN 978-1-7326470-2-2 (paperback, color)
ISBN 978-1-7326470-1-5 (hardcover)
Library of Congress Control Number: 2018954324

Published by Bessie's Story, LLC

www.bessiesstory.com

*Dedicated to **Rumsey Hall School**. I was fortunate to have experienced the magic of this place and its people.*

Table of Contents

Before We Begin 1

1. Time Remaining 3

2. Supplements 7

3. Hope 11

4. Halloween 15

5. Perspective 19

6. Hot Chocolate 23

7. Snowmen 29

8. Houseguests 33

9. New Tricks 39

10. Weekends 45

11. Spring Training 51

12. A Night Out 55

13. Back in the Water 59

14. Graduation 65

15. Summer Vacation: Part One 71

16. Summer Vacation: Part Two 75

17. Wounded 91

18. Back in School 95

19. Annual Checkup 101

20. Ice Hockey 105

21. Instincts Take Over 109

22. Barking at the Dark 113

23. Catching a Buzz 119

24. She's Upstairs Again 123

25. Right-Eyed Bessie 127

26. Cotton Balls 133

27. A Retriever Forever 139

28. Talking to Dogs 143

29. Angel's Halo 147

30. Love the One You're With 153

31. Watching the Lights Go Out 159

Postscript 165

Acknowledgements 167

About the Author 169

Before We Begin

When my wife, Ashley, and I visited the kennel in a rural New Hampshire town to select a chocolate Labrador puppy we had some reservations. The parents of the litter were described as healthy purebred Labs, but the mother was mysterious, aloof and detached, not to mention that her hair was falling out. The father was out of the picture, apparently having disappeared like a deadbeat dad who had slipped out of town before the police arrived.

Then the kennel's owner opened the small pen and eight adorable Lab puppies poured out, slipping and sliding all over each other like fish from a net. All except one. The last pup peered out at us, inched her way into the sunlight and parked herself softly on Ashley's feet. That's the day we fell in love with Bessie. She was just seven weeks old and we already knew we had the perfect dog. This book begins four years later when Bessie's perfection began rising to new levels.

CHAPTER 1

Time Remaining

The afternoon knows what the morning never suspected.—Robert Frost

Turning sixty-one was a wonderful surprise. Simple pleasures were magnified, I became a better listener, judgments were forgotten and forgiven, and I talked less because there was really not much point. By sixty-one a person has experienced most of the personal and universal joys and heartaches life can serve up, either directly or with one degree of separation. By sixty-one you get it, or you should. There's a faint drumbeat in the room when a person passes sixty. It's called TR, Time Remaining. You realize how quickly time has passed between forty and sixty, and understand that by some esoteric law of physics the next twenty years will be a blur.

But even with all of this life experience I am stunned when Ashley returns from a routine visit to the veterinarian with unsettling news. Our silly four-year-old Bessie is losing her sight. According to her doctor this sweet dog will be blind in twelve months. She has something called progressive retinal atrophy, an inherited disease that causes a degeneration of the retinas and results in permanent blindness.

Impossible! Bessie can run down a batted ball 250 feet from home plate. From across a room she spots a peanut dropped in the corner at a cocktail party. She comes to a screeching halt when out of the corner of her eye she notices a squashed salamander on the side of the road. This dog has radar and yet in twelve months, according to her doctor, she'll be lights out, pitch-blackness blind. I cry when I look at her, and then I laugh because as with most things in her life beyond food, chasing balls or loving us, Bessie is wonderfully unconcerned.

The doctor speculates that she currently has approximately 85 percent of her vision in daylight and 50 percent when it's dark. On walks after sunset she bumps into things, stumbles occasionally and takes it slow. I had thought that was just Bessie's style, but now I know better. When the sun comes up she is fearless and full-speed. Yet with each morning walk I look for a hint of fading glory. Almost subconsciously I realize Bessie is my GPS for the coming years of advancing age.

The research Ashley has done tells us that without the proper support, understanding and guidance Bessie could become depressed as she sees less and less. This dog has *never* had a bad day and now she may become *depressed?* I doubt it. That gene's just not in her DNA. The book Ashley purchased about blind dogs also tells us we should bring Bessie with us when we go out so she doesn't feel abandoned. (Let's hope our favorite restaurant will buy this wisdom.) And we learn that Bessie will likely need to be accompanied when she leaves the house in order to sustain her confidence. Knowing Bessie as I do, none of this advice seems particularly relevant.

At the moment Bessie has a tennis ball in her mouth, imploring me with her bright eyes to throw it into the dark backyard. She will bound after the ball with enthusiasm, run past it several times and finally find it with her nose more than her eyes. She is coping with her life-changing transition seamlessly, with the poise and style of a dancer who can no longer hear the music but continues to move by habit and memory with complete grace. The melody is buried deep in her soul.

CHAPTER 2

Supplements

The best way to find out if you can trust somebody is to trust them.—Ernest Hemingway

L ast week Ashley took Bessie to visit a veterinary ophthalmologist, a specialist. No kidding, there are such people. I'd hoped our dog would come home wearing a new pair of designer glasses and our worries would be over. I imagined Bessie walking through the door with thick, Coke-bottle lenses fastened to her head by elastic bands, or sports glasses like the ones you see NFL running backs wearing behind their facemasks. After all, it's the twenty-first century. There must be such things. But alas, even powerful lenses cannot repair the disappearing retinal tissue that is the root of Bessie's condition.

And so, like an aging professional baseball player from the steroid era, Bessie now takes a supplement. It's called Ocu-Glo, a blend of twelve natural pharmaceutical-grade antioxidants that work together to support the nutritional needs of a dog's eyes. Before each meal we jam a large, brown gelcap down her throat, which she swallows eagerly. It comes from us and she accepts it. Bessie would try to swallow a thumbtack if we asked her. That's how trusting she is.

I cannot help but think of a similar relationship professional baseball players Mark McGwire and Sammy Sosa may have had with their trainers. "Here, just take this. Trust me, it will improve your performance." So, we are going the supplement route. Not to solve the problem, just to slow it down. It's sort of like a commentary on the U.S. Government. Anything that's too unpleasant at the moment gets delayed or camouflaged. If it's not serious *today*, it's not serious. We fall into that same kind of thinking with our dear Bessie.

But you know what? I think the supplements are working! No kidding. Bessie actually seems to be seeing better now. She swerves to miss a tree at twilight, jumps over a log in her path and continues to stare at me with an eternal hope that she'll be rewarded with food or play. I'm sure she is looking right into my eyes, but there is an element of doubt there now. Just like those fading superstars: once in a while they hit one into the seats and the hope returns, but the strikeouts come too often and eventually the superstars get traded.

We will never trade Bessie. At the age of four and a half she is already in our Dog Hall of Fame, her number retired along with the other greats that preceded her. King, Beaver, Tucker and Bow round out the quintet of Super Dogs that let us live with them. Just a few months ago Ashley and I decided that Bessie might just be the best dog we've ever owned, except we don't really own Bessie anymore. She owns us now.

CHAPTER 3

Hope

The present is the ever-moving shadow that divides yesterday from tomorrow. In that lies hope.
—Frank Lloyd Wright

We decide to take Bessie on her first road trip since the diagnosis of eventual, certain blindness. She hops into the back seat of our car in Connecticut and three hours later bounds into an open meadow in New Hampshire where we own an 1840s farmhouse. It's been a month since she last visited the Granite State and I wonder if things look different to her. Apparently not. She exhibits all of her usual enthusiasm, sniffs around familiar places and barks beautifully to let the neighbors know that Hawkeye is back in town.

A change of scenery is good for the spirit. I wonder if Bessie feels the same stirrings of eternal youth in New Hampshire that our grown-up family experiences when we return to Nantucket Island each summer in August. We've notched thirty-three consecutive years visiting the island and it's always the same miracle. We get on the ferry in Hyannis, Massachusetts, weighed down by mainland worries and creaking, tired bodies, and disembark thirty miles out to sea feeling like carefree beach bums. The sights, sounds and smells of the island are like a facelift for our spirits.

I think it's the same for Bessie in New Hampshire because it's her birthplace and we spend most of our time outdoors when we're there. I take her to the nearby lake and toss a tennis ball thirty feet from shore. No hesitation! She plunges into the fifty-degree water, swims directly to the ball as if it's her dinner, and returns it to my feet with foggy, eager eyes that beg for another toss. If Bessie could talk she would say, "This is about as good as life can get. Throw it again." She might also say, "Why are you looking at me like that?" I hope I am sharp enough to understand when people look at me that way—the look that says, "You're losing it, but you don't know it." Hopefully, when that time comes I'll be as clueless and cheerful as Bessie, my mentor for aging gracefully.

I'm looking at her like that because I know she is slowly going blind. I'm looking at her like that because I know that eventually the ball I'm throwing will be just a splash in the lake. I wonder if she'll swim off after it into the empty, black water, hopeful, eternally hopeful, that her mouth and nose will find it. I pause, heartbroken at the thought of Bessie the Wonder Dog hearing the splash of the ball, plunging into the water and then stopping, or swimming in circles, confused and puzzled as to why it's always so dark at the lake now.

But today is all about hope. There's no question she seems sharper since the supplements kicked in; at least that's how it appears. I imagine that somehow we have a medical marvel here. Fueled by whatever edible organic morsels Bessie finds in her world, such as apples off the tree in our yard, roadkill, dead toads and worms, she will cure her condition and disprove her diagnosis. She'll be a canine Lance Armstrong beating the odds, leaving the doctors scratching their brilliant heads.

So we return from New Hampshire full of stupid hope until after dinner on Sunday night. I open the back door and watch Bessie run right into a potted mum on the porch as if it isn't there. I guess that's because for Bessie, it's not.

CHAPTER 4

Halloween

Learn the rules like a pro, so you can break them like an artist.—Pablo Picasso

Halloween is a pretty big deal in our house. We get a kick out of surprising little kids when they ring our doorbell looking for Ashley's famous chocolate chip cookies. These cookies are like gold on the child currency system, so the boys and girls in our neighborhood will do anything for them. They cautiously approach our front door with pounding hearts, shaking knees and watering mouths. The word has spread: these people are a little weird, but the cookies are worth it. The veterans in the group are wondering, "What do they have in store for us this year?"

Bessie has always been my barometer for costume design. If she lowers her tail, barks fiercely and backs away, it's a signal from a discerning judge that my get-up has passed the fright test. But this year when I approach her in full regalia her tail wags and she actually grins. She is happy to see me! She even licks my mask, another reminder that young Bessie's world is getting blurry. I feel sad, the same way I did that first Halloween when our sons Tyler and Trevor, both in their thirties now, were too cool to dress up. That was tough for a dad who still had lots of kid in him.

So I walk sullenly off to my post. This year we've parked our 1989 sedan right by the front door. When Ashley, dressed as a freakishly happy clown, holds out the tray of cookies, I, dressed as her twin, pop out of the trunk of our car like a jack-in-the-box. Several kids cry; most hide behind their parents. One brave little girl named Abby climbs into the trunk with me, cookie in hand. We give her an extra one.

In between visitors I lie in the trunk, in the dark, thinking mostly about Bessie and how she will never again be frightened by her foolish owner—another tradition fading. And I wonder when I will lose my zest for scaring trick-or-treaters. These thoughts are interrupted when I hear Ashley yelling, not in her fake, Halloween-scary voice, but her real-life scary voice, the one occasionally directed at me. *"Bessie, no! Stop that right now!"* Our vision-impaired dog has found the large plate of cookies in a pitch-black room and is savoring them. Like a lion that has separated a zebra from the herd, Bessie is feasting on her prey.

Maybe my mask really isn't that frightening this year. Or maybe, as the vet has told us, Bessie's hearing and sense of smell are becoming more acute as she compensates for her advancing blindness. Regardless, Bessie is banished to the mudroom for the rest of the trick-or-treating, in trouble again. And for the moment she is still our goofy, perpetually hungry, bright-eyed soul mate, acting completely normal.

CHAPTER 5

Perspective

In all affairs it's a healthy thing now and then to hang a question mark on the things you have long taken for granted.—Bertrand Russell

S ometimes in my job as Headmaster of a boarding school travel is required. In this case, six days to visit Seoul, South Korea—the Land of Morning Calm as it's referred to in travel brochures. South Korea is one of the friendliest, safest places I've ever been and its ancient culture promotes thoughtful reflection. You gain perspective in South Korea.

Being away from Bessie for almost a week, I ponder her condition on the flight home and wonder if her encroaching blindness will be more obvious upon my return, more dramatic than the gradual day-to-day transition that is my normal context. Will she recognize me or just stare with glazed eyes at this shape walking through the door smelling like kimchi, airline food and hotels? I figure since my scent has changed it will be a real test of Bessie's vision.

It's late at night when I return, so I quietly open the back door and enter the small area where she sleeps. It's after her bedtime and the noise wakes her. What does Bessie do? She smiles at me! The corners of her mouth curl up, her nose wrinkles and her grainy eyes sparkle as if to say, "Where have you been? I've been waiting for you." Clearly this dog recognizes me. Wonderful!

Believing that Bessie's blindness has been somehow put on hold, I find a tennis ball and head for the dimly lit backyard. This has become the new examination room, a litmus test for her eyesight. I throw the first ball off the porch and Bessie bounds after it, but not in the exact direction of the ball's path. Merely a misjudgment, I suspect. We try again. This time she somehow sees the movement of the yellow ball and takes off after it. The ball stops before she gets to it and now the impact of Bessie's condition is more obvious. She steps over the ball without noticing and unknowingly kicks it. Finally, after a couple minutes sniffing around, she grabs the ball in her mouth and heads proudly for the porch. Just before the step she stops, and then—well—like a blind person, she softly feels for the step up, her front paw like a white cane sensing a change in terrain.

Once back on the fully lit porch Bessie drops the prize at my feet. Her eyes have an iridescent glow now and she looks like a dog with artificial eyes, like some kind of Hollywood creation possessed of superpowers. It's almost frightening, actually, except that this is Bessie and she doesn't know how to frighten anything, except cats. She will run over hot coals, endure pricker bushes, even forfeit a meal to run a cat down or chase one up a tree.

That's it! When Bessie's blindness has advanced further, I'll get some cat owner to bring his feline by, place it in the backyard and open the door for Bessie. If she puts her nose up in the air, smells the cat and simply sits there, I'll know we've reached the danger zone. Until then, Bessie and I will just keep smiling at each other, and this courageous, wonderful companion will keep chasing tennis balls until she simply can't.

CHAPTER 6

Hot Chocolate

Remember then there is only one time that is important – Now! It is the most important time because it is the only time when we have any power.—Leo Tolstoy

The boarding school where we work and live is filled with wonderful seasonal traditions. One of our favorites occurs just before the students head home for the holiday season. Each grade comes to our house for Ashley's legendary hot chocolate with marshmallows and peppermint candy canes, a book reading and some storytelling. These class visits take place over a five-day period while students are preparing for exams. The best thing about traditions is that if you repeat the procedure each year, the only piece that changes is the age and wisdom of the participants. There are lots of "I remember when" moments as students recall previous visits at a younger age.

Bessie is crazy about traditions, especially those that involve food. The visits for hot chocolate ignite memories like firecrackers in a particular part of her small brain. It's laughable, really. We put on the Christmas music, prepare the cocoa and she has instant recall. Bessie knows that some careless kid will spill a drink, the marshmallows will roll under tables and chairs and she'll pick them off like a bat eating mosquitoes. She has an instinct for these things. Think of a horse in the starting gate at the Kentucky Derby. That's Bessie lining up for spilled hot chocolate or dropped marshmallows, with the occasional bonus of a candy cane.

Here's how it goes: Bessie freaks out as the preparations begin. The noises she makes are almost human—full of joy, nerves and drool. She remembers! We always put her in the mudroom when the kids arrive because she gets too excited and might hurt herself. This year we wonder what her reaction will be. Will the sounds and smells be enough to counterbalance her impaired vision? Foolish us. Of course they will. I swear that Bessie says the word "marshmallow" in the middle of a garbled sentence of dog talk. She is more excited than ever.

Off to the mudroom she goes: far be it from us to alter a tradition. As each gathering winds down Ashley opens Bessie's jail cell and she pours out onto the wooden floor, her legs slipping out from under her at the first turn like some cartoon character. In her world there is no one to collide with, no furniture to bump into, no rules at all really. With her nose to the ground she goes immediately to the place in the kitchen where the most marshmallows are dropped each year. Like a wily old prospector Bessie finds each nugget. Next stop, it's off to the sunroom where the students gather for storytelling. Bessie knows spills are likely to occur there, too.

From now on I'm going to put a few marshmallows in my wallet, on my key ring and with my cell phone. That way whenever I misplace these items, which is often, I will simply follow Bessie around until she tracks them down.

A thought passes through my head as I watch what is becoming a fifty-five pound olfactory lobe race through our house finding marshmallows. Bessie is subtly panicking. She knows, somehow, that next year the hot chocolate tradition will be different. She knows these might be the last marshmallows she'll ever *see*. Not the last she will ever eat. Oh no, that day is a long way off. But our nutty dog knows enough to savor this hunt with Bing Crosby singing "White Christmas" in the background.

How often do we say things like, "I can't wait until next week or next year"? Now I'm not thinking that way. With our canine vacuum cleaner as inspiration I am treasuring *this* year, *this* day, *this* moment. There may not be a next year or a next anything. This goofy, very good dog is bringing clarity to my world as hers becomes fuzzier and foggier. And here I thought she only cared about marshmallows.

CHAPTER 7

Snowmen

What is a friend? A single soul dwelling in two bodies.—Aristotle

S uddenly, winter has arrived, though the calendar says it's still autumn. According to some experts we are suffering from global warming, but you'd never know it looking out our window. There are six inches of snow on the ground and the temperature is in the twenties. Bessie likes the snow. The brightness of it appeals to her, the world suddenly turned on like some giant LED light bulb.

I've noticed a change in her eyes lately. Not only are they taking on a greenish glow like the eyes of a housefly; her pupils are perpetually enlarged. I understand that this allows maximum light to hit those decaying retinas, but the effect is that she looks like she has a permanent concussion, as if she is a little dazed. Eventually I suspect her eyes will be all pupils with no iris showing. She'll just have two black holes like a snowman's eyes.

For some reason I remember Ashley reading that we have to be aware of Bessie's possible depression as her blindness accelerates. It makes sense that a companion might help, so Bessie and I venture outside and build...a snowman for her to bark at. This snowman has two charcoal briquettes for eyes and they look very much like Bessie's. Here's the crazy part: I'm sure Bessie and the snowman make eye contact. Staring at her new best friend she seems to be saying, "You poor thing. At least I can see enough to find my way back into the house. You're stuck out here for good." Then she somehow notices that the snowman's ears and teeth are made of dog cookies.

Bessie checks on her new best friend periodically every day now. She sits by his side like a loyal pal. A warm spell hits and Frosty starts to wither and shrink. Bessie's reaction? She's been anticipating that the ears and teeth will fall out and be hers to enjoy. Somehow she figures these things out. I can't help wondering: as Ashley and I begin to wither and melt with advancing age, will our sons be like Bessie, waiting hopefully for treats?

Note to self: Let our sons Tyler and Trevor know at some point soon what will happen when we melt. Communicate what's in the final will and testament and settle that issue in advance so we'll know the motives for their visits in our old age are pure.

Bessie and I now have a new activity to supplement ball chasing—snowman building. I ask her, "Do you want to build a *snowman*?" and Bessie freaks out. Her one-track thinking does the translation: *snowman means cookies*. It may be my imagination, but Bessie seems to be watching the sky now, hoping for snow. This dog amazes me. She has a relatively small brain, but the temporal lobes, the parts that remember things, are extraordinarily well developed, especially when food is involved.

I even sense that Bessie is a bit upset with me. Her furrowed brow implores, "Why did you wait four years before showing me this whole snowman thing? Why did you wait until I was going blind?" You see, a snowman is hard to smell, and for a dog whose lights are going out body odor is a crucial factor in locating friends. But, as with all things, Bessie forgives me. There is just too much love in her heart for any sustained emotion except joy—pure, unbridled joy. And now she has a new snowman friend to share that with.

CHAPTER 8

Houseguests

What a hell of a heaven it will be when they get all these hypocrites assembled there!—Mark Twain

The holidays have passed, thank goodness, and Bessie is settling into somewhat of a winter routine. We've been cross-country skiing and snowshoeing together and she loves the idea that the world is permanently white now. Wherever we go she seems to be on the lookout for snowmen, and every time she becomes aware of one she assumes it's her buddy, runs to his side and waits for cookies. It's really quite hilarious. I guess they all look the same to her.

During the winter it is dark when Bessie wakes up and dark before dinner. That means there are fewer bright hours to each day. The book on blind dogs warned us, and

I'm beginning to think there's something to the suggestion that Bessie may be getting depressed over her changing universe. She just looks so terribly sad sometimes. And Bessie being Bessie, it's not sadness for herself she feels, but a sadness that seems to say, "I'm sorry I can't be the dog you thought I'd be." It's a look that just breaks my heart. So, like good, caring owners we arrange for Bessie to have some houseguests, a sleepover to take her mind off her plight.

Her two best canine friends happen to be Tula and Tui, the dogs owned by our sons. Both are female. Tula is a seasoned Pit Bull mutt from Brooklyn. Our older son, Tyler, rescued her as a puppy during his college days when the couple who owned her broke up and couldn't decide who would take the dog. Tula spent multiple hours a day chained to a post by a Fort Greene brownstone until our son adopted her. She has the Venus symbol for woman tattooed on her stomach. Tula was spayed as a puppy and this must have been a message to all of her suitors from Flatbush—"Save your ammo, boys." She wears it well.

Once a cheerful sweetheart, Tula is a bit crotchety now at eleven years old, grey in the face but still beautifully sleek, like some aging Hollywood star who spends hours each day with a personal trainer and a nutritionist and is friends with a cosmetic surgeon. You know, the type who looks great from a distance but more like something from a wax museum up close. Tula is a sweetie, but her demeanor can convey a strong sense of entitlement.

Our other guest is Tui, a Border Collie named after a large honey-eating bird of New Zealand where she was born. Our younger son, Trevor, traded a cord of firewood for Tui in Wanaka on the South Island where he spent a year after college. She flew home with him to New York and after almost two days of air travel in a crate, she walked out of baggage claim and pooped and peed in the terminal at JFK. I liked her right away.

Tui is a genius, bred to herd sheep, hundreds of them, all by herself. If there were colleges for dogs Tui would get a scholarship to all of the Ivies and Stanford. Simply stated, she loves all people and hates all other animals except Bessie. That's because Bessie lets Tui do *anything* to her, including dragging her around by the scruff of her neck. Sometimes I just have to turn away.

Both of our sons live nearby. On this particular weekend Tula's owner Tyler, the son who attended college in Brooklyn, went snowboarding with a pal in the mountains of Vermont. And Tui's owner Trevor, the son who attended college in the mountains of Colorado, went to a party with friends in New York City. Go figure. The result was that our house was dominated by dogs and Bessie loved it. Bessie is simply the most accommodating creature you will ever meet. She gives up her bed to Queen Tula and drops balls at Tui's feet. If there was just one bowl of food Tula would expect it, Tui would fight for it and Bessie, who usually lives to eat, would get out of the way.

Over the weekend Ashley and I go for long walks with the dogs, wrestle with them, build another snowman, watch football games, nap—you know, regular January things. And as the hours pass I realize that Bessie, the youngest, is acting like the oldest. She thoughtfully relents to everything, like a lost breed of politician who knows how to compromise and get along with diverse groups. This trio of dog characters meshes like a three-part harmony because Bessie defers. I don't think it's insecurity or lack of confidence that makes Bessie behave this way. She is like a Buddha who has found enlightenment and simply wants others to be happy and content.

Here she is at the age of four losing her eyesight day by day and these older fools are worrying about who sleeps where and who gets the cookies. Once again this humble dog shines a bright light on our world from her increasingly dark one. Her message: *Wake up!*

Ninety-nine percent of the things we do each day are of little or no importance. The only things that really matter are those we do to make life a little better for others. I wish Bessie could look in a mirror and see how beautiful she is. That is not going to happen, but somehow I think she knows she is getting lovelier by the day. You can see it in her eyes.

CHAPTER 9

New Tricks

You don't become inactive because you age, you age because you become inactive.—Anonymous

I t's February and we've had snow on the ground since November. What's more, the groundhog saw his shadow so we are in for six more weeks of winter. This has really put a damper on Bessie's unquenchable desire to run down batted or thrown balls. With the inevitable day approaching when her lights will go out, I feel compelled to find some new seasonal activities for her. I imagine being blind is like endlessly dreaming. Since Bessie will associate sounds and smells with her most recent visual memories, they must be vivid. It's my responsibility to create these memories for her.

After yet another substantial snowfall I am finishing up shoveling the walkways and cleaning snow off the cars. We've got this routine now where every other shovelful of snow gets thrown on Bessie. She bites at it, rolls around in it and bounces up with her face covered in the white stuff. This must soothe some sort of winter dry skin condition for her because she *loves* it. This new game doesn't replace ball chasing, but I know Bessie likes it because when I pick up the shovel she convulses with joy.

One day I do a little experiment: I put the shovel in the snow, and about three feet away place a bat and ball. It's her choice. Predictably, Bessie chooses the bat and ball. Winter's okay, but this dog is ready for spring training. And since pitchers and catchers report to their respective training camps around this time of year, it makes sense that we should probably begin our own type of pre-season drills, assuming and hoping Bessie's fading vision won't keep her off the team this year.

But how do you hit fungoes in a foot or more of snow? Bessie solves this problem herself. While walking toward the house after shoveling one day I find my path blocked by you-know-who with a partially deflated soccer ball in her mouth. The ball is bigger than Bessie's head, so she really looks quite comical. The message is clear, though. She had retrieved the ball from some bushes next to the soccer field that abuts our house. I can almost imagine Bessie thinking, "It's round, big and it fits in my mouth. I wonder if...?"

At first it isn't clear what Bessie has in mind. Then she drops the ball at my feet and does a quick back and forth flashing with her aging eyes. Her head shifts from the ball to me, back to the ball, then to me, then to the ball, then to me again. Suddenly, I get what she is trying to say. "Let's use this ball until the snow melts. It rolls on top of the snow and I'd have to be blind not to see it." Smart dog this Bessie, but perhaps a little bit in denial.

Now the soccer ball sits on our porch like a friend waiting for Bessie to come out and play. Here's how it goes: I kick or throw the ball down the driveway and it rolls into deeper snow. Its movement registers somewhere on Bessie's receptors and she charges after it. Once she's located the ball she pounces on this semblance of prey, grabs it in her mouth and shakes the hell out of it. After she's properly 'broken its neck' she brings it back, drops it at my feet and the back and forth looks continue until the next launch. As soon as my motion begins Bessie heads off in the anticipated direction of the kick or throw, her confidence securely intact.

Sometimes the big ball comes to rest before Bessie gets close to it. This is the saddest thing to watch, the ball just inches away as she moves right past it or walks into it. I wonder, is that why the most elderly among us sit so calmly much of the time? Does the world have less motion later on in life, or do we slow it down so there is less to anticipate? Again this fearless, rapidly aging dog with uncommon wisdom lights the way for a slowly aging sport. Her message: keep moving, and keep the world around you moving, too.

CHAPTER 10

Weekends

As long as habit and routine dictate the pattern of living, new dimensions of the soul will not emerge.
—Henry Van Dyke

Bessie loves routines. Hers are ironclad. For example, her response every morning when I open the door to the mudroom where she sleeps is *exactly* the same. She bolts past me, skitters on the wood floors of the kitchen and stops just before smacking into the swinging door that separates the kitchen from the area where the back door is located. I guess I'll know when Bessie is blind because she'll run into the swinging door instead of stopping. For now, in early March, she squirms and whines and flaps her tongue until I let her out. She does the exact same 360-degree whirling dervish spin, jumps on and off the porch, and then bounds off in pursuit of whatever bird or squirrel may be foolish enough to hang around the bird feeder. It's so predictable I sometimes think she could do this blindfolded, and I guess we'll find out eventually.

When Bessie wants to come back in she sits like a dog angel by the door and waits patiently, knowing her breakfast is being prepared. As a puppy she ate her food so fast it was unhealthy. The vet told us to slow her down by putting a softball in her bowl. Now, she won't eat *unless* the ball is in the bowl. No kidding. We put the bowl down in front of her, tell her it's okay, but she will not eat until we place the ball in her bowl. Routine is important to Bessie. This will be another test of her declining vision, if she eats without the ball.

After her breakfast Bessie comes over to the table where I'm eating and puts her head in my lap. I take a minute to scratch her face hard and rub her eyes before she lies down in the adjacent room where she can keep an eye on me, the same routine every day like clockwork. But here's the crazy part: I wear a coat and tie to work, six days a week. On Sundays I eat breakfast in pajamas and Bessie notices. I'm sure of it because instead of lying down after her face scratch and eye rub, she backs off a few steps and starts to mumble. Somehow she knows I will not be heading off for the day and in her mind that means we can play. She finds her ball and pesters me like a spoiled child until I take her outside.

How can this be for a dog who is going blind? Don't all humans basically look the same to dogs, especially dogs with fading vision? Does Bessie really check out what I am wearing each day? Apparently so, because this canine fashionista knows her routine changes on Sundays, just like mine, and the only difference at the start of the day is what I am wearing. When Bessie was a clear-eyed puppy who could climb stairs, she would gently take my shoe from the closet and place it by the door, a message that she wanted to go for a walk. I wonder now, if

Bessie still climbed stairs, would she rip all of my neckties into shreds in hopes that would keep me home?

How wonderful that Bessie understands and loves the concept of weekends. Here I'd been thinking that in a dog's life Wednesdays, Mondays and Sundays were all the same. Not so. Some strange circadian rhythm is at work in her mind. I wonder, what will her life be like when she can no longer see what I am wearing and all days look the same? Knowing Bessie, she'll probably sense the different sound my slippers make on the floor compared to shoes. Or she'll smell the sleep in my pajamas rather than the cotton, wool or corduroy of my pants. Somehow this dog will know the difference between a workday and a playday.

Bessie has done it again, teaching me that while routines have their function, it's important to get off the cement truck sometimes and find new ways to perceive the world. And she helps me understand that there is *always* a way to find joy and have some fun.

Sometimes you have to close your eyes to see it.

CHAPTER 11

Spring Training

"What day is it?"
"It's today," squeaked Piglet.
"My favorite day," said Pooh.
—A. A. Milne

March rolls around, and with it daylight savings stretches the end of each day. Suddenly Bessie is rejuvenated. The snow on the field adjacent to our house melts, robins and swallows return and baseball is back in the sports pages. Bessie must notice all of this because each time we let her out the side door she runs to the shed where the bats and balls are stored. It's spring training time! She wants to impress the coach and make the team.

I have been scrutinizing Bessie's declining eyesight, and either she has developed

tremendous compensatory skills or this resilient dog has stalled the decay of her retinas. In fact, there seems to be evidence that
her vision is improving. Go figure. She is running down batted balls like an energetic rook-
ie, changing directions like a shortstop on a
bad hop. Her peripheral vision defies logic
and Bessie's understanding of the game seems
deeper. We had a friend take care of Bessie
while we were away for a few days and
upon our return she told us that if we hadn't
pointed out Bessie's diminished eyesight, she
probably wouldn't have noticed.

But alas, I think our girl's problems are
micro right now, rather than macro; Bessie's
ability to see things at a distance seems to
be fading less quickly than her ability to see
things up close. When I play catch with her
at close range, tossed balls bounce off her
forehead. If the ball drops in front of her
she will walk around it and appear to look
right at it without noticing. When Ashley and
I have been away for a while, we walk in the
house and Bessie stares at us with a blank

look on her face, not sure who we are until she can sniff us or hear our voices. And that strange green glow in her eyes is intensifying.

To better understand Bessie's plight, I put on sunglasses one dark evening and walk through our backyard. It is frightening, really. The farther I get from familiar objects, the more I bump into things and the harder it is to negotiate my path. I throw a ball into the darkness and can't find it. The urge to remove the sunglasses is overpowering, and it affords me another chance to admire how stoically Bessie is coping.

Okay, I think I get it. Bessie's joy and enthusiasm are fueled by the prolonged daylight the change of seasons brings. That means we are in the very early stages of her final, joyous spring during which she can still see. Next year, April and December will look the same to Bessie. Christmas and Easter will be indistinguishable. I'm holding out hope that somehow, Bessie the all-star will have another great season in her bag of tricks, a final hurrah before her inevitable retirement and existential move to a condo village in Florida.

Knowing that this pipe dream of rejuvenation is unlikely, I find myself being more in the moment. When Bessie comes to me with a ball in her mouth I am more likely now to drop what I'm doing and give her what she wants—my time. I recall feeling somewhat the same way with our children when they were young and asked me to play catch or go fishing. I knew the day would come when they'd outgrow their interest in being with Dad, so I almost always said yes. With Bessie it's different. Her ability will disappear before her interest fades and I can only imagine how terribly confusing and heartbreaking that will be for her. So here I am again, always saying yes.

I tend to see everyone in my life now as I see Bessie. That is, in the bright, shining light of the moment. The celebration of today is all I can be sure of. Bessie teaches me: *be where you are.*

CHAPTER 12

A Night Out

When nature made you, they broke the mold—rumor has it they beat the hell out of the mold-maker, too.
—Anonymous

Bessie has the position of things outside our house pretty well memorized. Porch furniture, bushes, trees, steps, fences, stone walls, potted plants, parked cars; these permanent fixtures are seared in her memory, stored on her hard drive like some computer app. You know how you somehow remember the lyrics to a favorite song from your teenage years, even if you haven't heard it for decades? Bessie's memory of the area surrounding our house is like that. It's the unexpected obstacles that give her the most trouble.

One Saturday we are raking the front yard, cleaning up the thatch and twigs that have been hiding under five endless months of snow on the ground. The small piles of seasonal debris are left behind like the trash after a party that went on way too long. We pick up winter's residue and place it in a wheelbarrow next to the driveway. Bessie runs right into the darn thing and knocks it over. If one of our kids had done this twenty years ago I'd have been upset. But with Bessie, I just laugh, and then comfort her. The poor girl is just so startled that this *thing* has been installed haphazardly in her well-known path. She can't figure out where it came from or what it is.

While patting her I wonder if getting old might be like this. Do we consciously make sure we are in predictably safe places and situations all the time so we don't bump into things or ideas that are unfamiliar?

That night we are invited to a friend's house for supper. As I've said, the book on blind dogs recommends that Bessie be included in various outings so she does not get depressed and feel abandoned as her visual world shrinks. So Ashley decides at the last minute to bring Bessie with us rather than leave her home alone. The evening is going fine until after dinner when Bessie signals that she needs to go for a walk. As we head out our friend's back door onto the porch, Bessie walks into a chair. I help her negotiate a step down onto the patio and then she walks headfirst into a boxwood hedge. There she is, standing still with her head fully immersed in the hedge, looking like some sort of silly sculpture by a demented artist. In her bright-eyed youth Bessie might have willingly put herself in this position to track down a small bird or squirrel. But on this night it's accidental.

I fight the urge to rescue her and simply say, "No, girl." She backs up, noses along the hedge and eventually senses the steps that lead to the open yard. She navigates the small lawn carefully, often hesitating before moving ahead. The lights from our host's windows must be like distant lighthouses for Bessie because she seems to always keep them in her fuzzy field of vision. After a few minutes I call her back and watch as she thoughtfully works her way to my voice, scraping a few bushes along the way. She gingerly manages the two steps onto the patio and then hits her shin on the porch, which is one step higher. No complaints or anguish, just a careful lady coping. My God, I hope I can age with that same courage, grace and dignity.

Back inside Bessie is rewarded with cookies, her big black eyes twinkling with joy, drool dripping off her chin. "Don't," I think to myself, "become afraid of new things." Be like Bessie: As long as you can move, keep moving. Avoid getting stuck in familiar patterns and for goodness sake don't make your world so familiar that you can manage it blindfolded. And if at the end of even the smallest new adventure you drool when you eat your cookies, that's okay. Friends and loved ones will understand.

CHAPTER 13

Back in the Water

And the beauty of a woman, with passing years only grows!—Audrey Hepburn

We own a tiny, rickety, but charming hundred-year-old cottage on a small lake just a mile away from our farmhouse. We've named the place *Tucked In* because the cozy shack is snuggled in a cove. Thankfully, the waterfront provides an illusion of space and grandeur. The last time we checked on it in March there were still eighteen inches of snow on its sagging roof. As we drive down the dirt road in May to open the cottage for the season Ashley and I wonder if the little gem will still be standing. Thankfully, it has survived. Bessie is happy, too.

When we are at the lake Bessie divides most of her time between swimming after tennis balls and sleeping in the sun. She also likes to ride in our thirteen-foot Boston Whaler and stand on the nose of our paddleboard surveying the lake homes from the water as I paddle her around. At least she did last year. So we are wondering how she will handle these traditional activities seven months after her diagnosis. Bessie smells the lake before she sees it, so she's mentally prepared. Without hesitation she leaps out of the car and instinctively makes her way to the water's edge to get her bearings.

We have one of those Chuckit devices, a flexible plastic gadget about three feet long with a cup at the end that holds a tennis ball. When you snap the Chuckit your arm speed is magnified and the ball jets skyward. Bessie knows this game well. When the tennis ball is loaded she plunges into the water and swims in the direction she expects the ball will travel. Every fiber of her body is keyed into locating the splash.

On the first throw we anticipate the worst, thinking that Bessie might just swim around aimlessly. I don't know how, but once she hears the splash she's off to the races, shifting gears in the water like a hungry shark sensing a wounded fish flopping on the surface. She zeroes in on the tennis ball with laser precision, snaps it up in her mouth and swims back to shore, beaming like an Olympic champion, delighted that her compensatory skills can extend her career retrieving balls. Her eyes twinkle with a brightness that proclaims, "I've still got it."

On each successive chuck I send the ball farther out in the water and each time Bessie tracks it down, as long as she can sense the splash. To verify this I send a ball at a right angle to Bessie's single-minded track. Sure enough, she doesn't find it and has to be called back, empty-mouthed and deeply confused. But the joy returns with the next well-placed chuck.

The ride on the paddleboard is also a success of sorts. Last year I paddled up to the dock, Bessie hopped on board and off we went. This year when I bring the board to the dock she just tilts her head at me. "Are you crazy?" she seems to say with her expression. It's as if I am asking her to jump out of a third-story window. So we adjust. I guide her onto the board and off we go.

On past journeys around the lake Bessie would scout out the cookouts and then, returning home, she would sneak back along the shore and visit the houses where the burgers smelled best. On this spring day the lake is quiet, but she sticks her hopeful nose up in the air and sniffs deeply, perched on the end of the board like a fancy hood ornament on some fashionable car. It's a short journey to test her balance and she performs with sure-footed confidence.

As we drive back to Connecticut on Sunday Bessie sleeps soundly, snoring in the back seat, happy that at least for the time being summer will be summer again. And I am having similar thoughts. As long as we are willing to compensate for the gradual decline that accompanies the privilege of aging, we can continue to enjoy modified versions of our favorite activities. It's only May and I am psyched.

CHAPTER 14

Graduation

All real education is the architecture of the soul.—William Bennett

A t our school, as at most boarding schools, graduation is a deeply emotional experience. I know this is the case at public schools and independent day schools to some extent, but at boarding school it's intensified. People live together at boarding school and graduation is the end of that. After you've shared meals, weekends, triumphs and tragedies, you name it, there is sadness at the end of a school year that has to be experienced to be understood. Imagine your kids going off to college forever, never to return. That's graduation at a boarding school. It's goodbye on steroids. The day after graduation is the saddest day of the year for me.

Bessie loves graduation week. Our house is the location for all sorts of special events. With senior class dinners, family receptions, faculty parties and other gatherings there is an ongoing parade of people through our home. For Bessie that means lots of food dropped on the floor. Never mind that she spends an inordinate amount of time in the mudroom during graduation week. Bessie knows that eventually she will be set free from her purgatory of listening to and smelling the party and be allowed to participate. When the door to the mudroom is opened it's like a fox hunt.

When Bessie could see, she would casually meander around the house on a visual tour of places where food collected, accepting pats on the head from those annoying folks who like to be the last to leave a party. Now, Bessie seems possessed in her treasure hunt. Because she can't see very well, it's a nose-to-the-ground, antisocial endeavor. She bumps into people and bangs into furniture, always with her nose skimming the floor in search of morsels that she used to spot from twenty yards away but now can only smell.

The students know Bessie is losing her sight and forgive her, but the parents, like all parents, are more judgmental. They can't believe our dog has no manners. I can only imagine their comments on the car ride home—"I hope our children aren't given free reign at school like that guy's dog is." Maybe we should get Bessie a sign that she can wear around her neck: *Going blind, please be patient.*

It's interesting to watch our sweet food-detective survey a room after a party. In the old days Bessie knew what a dropped hors d'oeuvre looked like. Now everything is a potential snack: toothpicks, napkins, shoes, leaves. From Bessie's perspective any object is a vague, blurry piece of food until it can be sniffed. She still loves the search, but it's transitioning into a sort of frantic desperation. It's sad, really, very sad.

The pace of life quickens as graduation approaches. I am constantly running in and out of our house. Life is a blur. Each time I race through the door I look for Bessie and she looks for me. It's not the knowing, happy look that greeted me the first five years of her life. Now, it's a puzzled, searching, longing look. She's not sure it's me and needs a touch and a sniff to identify who's there. Or a voice—a voice always helps. And Bessie snuggles into corners now. She likes the feeling of small places with walls close by. The other day I walked in unexpectedly and she was lying in a space between the couch and a chair. It couldn't have been more than a two-foot-square area and tough to negotiate. But there she was, peering out at me from the tiny opening of her self-imposed cell, comforted by the coziness of this new space she'd discovered.

I wish I could capture in words the expression on Bessie's face, the eerie gleam of her eyes. "I'm scared," she seemed to be saying. "I don't know what's happening, but the world is changing...fast. Please take care of me and don't stop loving me."

I stopped in my tracks, sat on the couch and put Bessie on my lap. She licked my face and conveyed a love and appreciation that defy belief. I hope when I am more difficult to love the people close to me put me on their laps, tell me they understand and let me kiss them. For Bessie, that seemed to take the fear away and her joy returned.

CHAPTER 15

Summer Vacation
Part One

You can easily judge the character of a man by how he treats those who can do nothing for him.
—Malcolm Forbes

After school ends in mid-June Ashley, Bessie and I head off for two weeks of vacation at our lake cottage. This is the start of summer for us and Bessie loves it because we have more time for her. To add some spice, the three of us journey to the White Mountains for a couple days of hiking. This may be the last time Bessie will be able to tackle some of the more challenging trails, so we decide to push her a little bit.

On the first day Bessie handles the toughest terrain like a Sherpa who forgot his glasses, leaping across rocky gaps by instinct and gleefully bounding up the steepest terrain with only a few stumbles. At the summit Ashley and I take turns holding her back as we make the final climb to the highest rocky point. Bessie whines and whimpers like a rambunctious child, not understanding why she is under wraps. Since no one bothered to inform her that she is losing her eyesight, she heads into dangerous situations with inappropriate confidence. Consequently we feel we have to protect her from herself. It's becoming a concern.

The first night at the mountain inn where we stay Bessie bunks in the car with the windows cracked open. Around eight that evening we hear her distinctive bark as we enjoy a well-earned cocktail. Like curious parents we peer off the inn's porch at sunset and see a black bear wandering past our car in the parking lot. I don't exactly know how Bessie processes what is happening because by now her vision is so impaired that the bear can only be an indistinct moving shape with a new odor, but Bessie knows it doesn't belong there and she is warning us. After we reassure her with a personal visit to affirm our safety, Bessie is down for the night in the back seat, confident she has scared the bear away.

The next day we hike to the famous Tuckerman's Ravine. This trail starts gently, and then quickly becomes a challenging, endless climb up what is best described as a steep, rocky staircase. Ashley and I hike at different speeds, and Bessie moves back and forth between us during the climb like some high-priced trail guide making sure we are both safe. It's touching to see her peer back at a turn in the trail, her nose pointed upward, sniffing to check on the slower hiker. She waits until she is positive it's one of us before resuming her trek, always the caretaker. My goodness, I love this dog.

Occasionally we encounter a group of hikers and Bessie becomes quite anxious. To her we all look the same, so she frantically runs around sniffing people, searching for a familiar scent. One particular group is from Quebec and does not speak English. The poor thing is beside herself with worry that she's somehow lost us and we are gone forever. The sounds and accents of the French language confuse her even more and Bessie panics. Confident that she will find us by our scent, we let her solve this problem on her own. Finally, she picks us out of the crowd and her eager summit quest resumes.

Bessie absolutely loves this two-day sojourn. In the back seat on the way home she sleeps like a baby, dreaming about her adventures and quivering with glee. I, on the other hand, am haunted by my vivid memory of the fear on her face when she thought that somehow she had lost us in the sea of strangers. I've seen a similar look of panic on elderly people when they are temporarily confused or feel abandoned, but this was different. Bessie's fear was not that we had lost her and she would be alone. Rather, she was afraid she had lost us and had failed to do her job as protector. There is a big difference.

CHAPTER 16

Summer Vacation
Part Two

My dear girl, you must cultivate a taste for the finer things. Civilized pleasures give meaning to life.
—Barbara Taylor Bradford

During the summer I live a split life. Weekdays are spent on the job in Connecticut, taking care of business. On the weekends I head for the cottage in New Hampshire to join Ashley and Bessie. The time away each week provides perspective on the pace of Bessie's creeping blindness. I'd describe her decline as slow and steady, like snow melting in March. One of the indicators is that she is quicker to bark at all things that move or make sounds. When I pull up late Friday afternoon, Bessie senses someone getting out of the car and lets out a robust, warning bark. As my voice and scent become obvious she smiles and wrinkles up her nose with glee. Then she runs to get her new toy. Same routine every Friday.

For some personal, private reason Bessie loves Ashley more than me. If all three of us are standing in the middle of a field and Ashley and I walk in opposite directions, Bessie will *always* go with Ashley. It may go back to that day when we first selected her at the kennel, when Bessie lay down on Ashley's feet—love at first sight, I guess. Over the years I've tried hard to turn her my way, to no avail. But I am better at playing with Bessie so I let her use me at her discretion.

We purchased a new toy for Bessie, a brilliant orange cylinder about a foot long with a string tied to one end. It makes a louder splash than a tennis ball and is easier for her to locate. When she knows the game is on Bessie drops the toy at my feet, plunges into the lake and swims for deeper water. I swing the toy by its string and toss it in the direction she is swimming. Bessie senses the splash and retrieves it like—well—like a Labrador retriever. Every Friday, on that first throw of her toy the cumulative impact of the relentless invasion on her retinas becomes clear. It's heartwarming that her facial expressions are the same and her energy and spirit are intact, but her eyesight is slipping fast.

Darkness has become a heartless villain. We have to keep an eye on Bessie now or she might break something or injure herself. The other night she ran full speed into our car, bounced off, and continued her quest after some phantom object. Ashley suggests we put her on a leash at night, but I'm holding off on that for now. I'll deal with the hassle, sort of like talking at a louder volume when a loved one is hard of hearing. I did that with my late mother-in-law and she laughed about it, good sport that she was. Our conversations took lots of ninety-degree turns.

One dark night I have an idea. Headlamp! I fashion a headlamp for Bessie so that the world directly in front of her will forever be high noon. After adjusting the straps to fit on the top of her head at the correct angle, out we go. It's pretty cool for about fifteen seconds. I know exactly where Bessie is and she can see what is right in front of her, I think. But Bessie has an uncanny knack for removing anything from her face that doesn't belong there. The headlamp must feel like a giant spiderweb wrapped around her head. She tears it off with her paws without a thought. Vision be damned. She wants to go au naturel.

Our shower at the cottage is a two-and-a-half gallon black vinyl bag with a little nozzle at the bottom. We fill the bag with water in the morning, place it in a sunny spot and have hot water in just a few hours. We hoist the bag up an old birch tree by a pulley and the platform we stand on is at nose level for Bessie. When she was younger and could see, before she stopped climbing stairs, she loved to hang out by the tub and lick soap off us when we bathed. I'd forgotten this until one evening when I am soaping up under the solar shower, eyes closed, daydreaming blissfully and almost jump out of my skin. Bessie has snuck up on me and is licking the soap off my feet. After the initial shock wears off I realize it feels kind of nice. Now, when we take showers in the pine trees outside the back door, having our feet licked is a standard part of the experience. Bessie loves it, and she smells like fresh soap and shampoo at the end of each day.

It's a classic win-win situation. We get the pleasant feeling of having our feet gently licked in the shower, and Bessie gets her daily soap fix. This is one treat absolutely unconnected to her eyesight. Since she does it with her eyes closed, Bessie can look forward to this simple joy for years to come. And so can we.

Bessie, seven weeks old, the day she joined our family.

Our adorable, blue-eyed puppy

One-year-old Bessie with her best friends, Tui and Tula

At two years old, Bessie loved the snow.

Age three and a half. Soon after this picture was taken Bessie was diagnosed with progressive retinal atrophy.

Bessie and I pause during a hike in the White Mountains of New Hampshire. At age four and a half we can tell her world is changing.

Bessie licking soap off my feet at the outdoor shower by our rustic lake cottage.

Marching in the Blue Dog Parade at age five, Bessie relies more and more on sounds and scents to find her way.

This is the day Bessie learned to play ice hockey. Approaching her sixth birthday, her pupils are perpetually dilated.

Bessie implores me with cloudy eyes to throw her soccer ball.

Fermented apples have become one of Bessie's favorite snacks.

Sightless by age six, Bessie poses with one of her pals.

With a little help and guidance, Bessie still loves to ride around the lake on a paddleboard.

Even though she is completely blind, Bessie continues to look straight into my eyes.

Using her nose, ears and instincts, Bessie has never stopped retrieving.

Despite her blindness, Bessie will not eat unless her ball is in the bowl.

At age nine Bessie is still happiest following her retriever instincts.

Bessie on the bow at age nine. Sunset cruises have been a favorite of hers since she was a puppy.

Bessie with Ashley and me

CHAPTER 17

Wounded

The oak fought the wind and was broken, the willow bent when it must and survived.—Robert Jordan

You may recall that Bessie's best canine friends are our sons' dogs—Tui, the genius, know-it-all Border Collie from New Zealand and Tula, the stylish, aristocratic Pit Bull mix from Brooklyn. The trio spend a week together when our aging family goes on our annual trip to Nantucket in August. Ashley and I met on the island in 1975 and we've gone back to the scene of the crime every year since. The pilgrimage to Nantucket has survived infant children, teenagers, college kids and now thirtysomethings. For a week we pretend we are the only non-dysfunctional family in America. It's really a fun time, but we all miss our dogs.

While we're away friends move into our on-campus house in Connecticut to take care of the pack for the week. Each year we get a phone call about halfway through the vacation with some minor pet emergency. This year, as we expected, the call is about Bessie. Our friends had taken the dogs for a walk in the nearby woods. Everybody was getting along just fine until Bessie, not being able to see clearly, ran into Tula. I guess Tula was fed up with Bessie's blindness because she turned around and bit Bessie on the ass, *hard.*

The bite opened up a hole about the size of a quarter. Photos of the injury are emailed to us and a collective diagnosis is made that a vet's services are not required. We subsequently learn that Bessie constantly licks the wound, preventing healing. Someone remembers that we have one of those plastic Elizabethan collars in the basement at home, left over from a previous wound. Like experienced veterinarians we prescribe that Bessie wear the contraption and go back to giving the vacation our full attention.

When we return home we realize the hardship our decision has caused. It's tough enough under normal conditions for Bessie to navigate around chairs, under tables and through doors. Put a large plastic cone around her head and the problem is magnified exponentially. The poor thing was slamming into furniture, getting stuck in doorways and knocking things over. Going outside at night was worse. It's a wonder she didn't break her neck. Our younger son described it as watching a friend who's had too much to drink running around at a party with a lampshade on his head.

The thing is, Bessie is a full-speed dog whether she can see or not. Even with a plastic cone around her neck and head she still wants to chase tennis balls. Who am I to dampen her enthusiasm? I launch the balls and Bessie heads off in the approximate direction, intent on satisfying her genetic predisposition. There she is, head completely hidden under the plastic cone as she sniffs around the backyard undaunted, searching for her ball.

Bessie's irrepressible spirit is evident when we examine her Elizabethan collar the day we remove it for good. It is cracked and chipped with streaks of paint on it, like the helmet of a middle linebacker at the end of a brutal season. That's our Bessie. She leads with her head, and she has a nice scar on her fanny to prove it.

I am waiting for something in Bessie's spirit to give way, like a prizefighter who sits on his stool in the corner shaking his head, refusing to come out for the last round. But now one year after her diagnosis, about the time when the doggie optometrist said she'd be lights out blind, Bessie is loving life more than ever. It dawns on me that I am a year older, too. Thanks to Bessie I laugh more than ever and savor the joy of all that I *can* do. I'm lucky this dog lives alongside me. She's become my very own seeing-eye dog by the most unusual set of circumstances.

CHAPTER 18

Back in School

Don't cry because it's over, smile because it hap-pened.—Dr. Seuss

Days are getting shorter and the school year is into its second month. October's colors are slowly fading and the messy season of falling leaves is upon us. Bessie is surrounded by kids and activity on the campus and the pace seems to have rejuvenated her. Not that she needs it, because her spirit has never really faded, not one little bit.

We live right next to the school's largest athletic field and every afternoon she hears soccer games, cross country races and the intoxicating noise of happy, active kids. Each time Ashley or I walk through the door Bessie implores us with glaring, glowing green eyes to let her out so she can join the fun.

When we do the kids surround her as if she conveys some secret power. Bessie emits a level of joy and energy that makes everyone around her a little happier. She has no reservations or self-doubts about her obvious weakness and I think middle school kids admire this in her, secretly wishing they could handle their own perceived flaws with the same carefree attitude and disposition.

A favorite fall tradition for Bessie is the Blue Dog Parade, an event that kicks off the year's interscholastic athletic competition. Our school mascot is the Blue Dog, so each fall the campus dogs are dressed up by their owners in school colors and walked through the campus to the cheers and applause of the students. Bessie wears her Elizabethan collar, but this time as a skirt, along with a school T-shirt and a stylish pink bow on the top of her head.

When we dress Bessie up for a rehearsal the night before the parade, I swear she recalls how this goes. I'm pretty sure that if she knew what she looked like she would resist, but she remembers that there are always treats offered after the parade, so she complies willingly. During the parade she bumps into people, walks unknowingly between kids' legs and generally loves the attention and pats from hands she can't really see. The parade ends as she hoped, with a handful of dog cookies.

A few days after the parade, with pleasant memories guiding her, Bessie follows a group of kids from the athletic fields about half a mile back to the main campus and eventually makes her way to the steps outside my office. She appears as if she is on vacation, has just landed at the airport and is waiting for a ride. Bessie spends about an hour sitting there picking up head scratches and hugs the way a street musician collects dollars and spare change from passersby for a well-played melody. I watch her from my office window for a while and smile at the grace she conveys surveying a landscape she can't really see, but understands.

We still take Bessie on walks in the woods and somehow she senses where the trail is; she just knows where to go. Wouldn't it be nice if we all had that inner sense of direction and knew just where to go with our lives? If you watch her in action from a distance you would never suspect she is almost sightless. Bessie is working from her core now, that part of her soul that seems to transcend the physical hardships. Or maybe her spirit just overpowers her grief.

Each morning when I awake it takes a little longer to loosen up, a few more steps before the stiffness eases. It's part of the simple, well-earned privilege of growing older. Sometimes I feel regret, but then I let Bessie out the back door and the contagious enthusiasm she exhibits storming into a new day inspires me.

For Bessie, the beginning of *every* day is like the start of a brilliant sun-kissed morning after a heavy rainstorm, when the world is scrubbed clean and filled with endless promise and freshness. She heads out that door each morning with the boundless high hopes and great faith—no, *blind* faith—that this will be the best day of her life. If Bessie could talk I'm pretty sure she'd simply say, "Be strong and spread joy." That's a pretty good message from a dog whose world is getting darker each day.

CHAPTER 19

Annual Checkup

There are only two forces in the world: the sword and the spirit. In the long run the sword will always be conquered by the spirit.—Napoleon Bonaparte

More than a year ago Bessie's doctor predicted that she would be completely blind by now. So when Ashley takes her to an appointment with the canine ophthalmologist after the start of school we know our girl has defied the original prognosis. Bessie can still see; we just don't know how much. Her decline is clearly evident, but blind dogs are wonderfully adaptive, especially when their loss of vision occurs gradually over time, like hair turning grey. You see a picture of yourself thirty years ago and marvel at how young you looked: the transformation has been so subtle it happens almost without notice. Bessie's blindness is like that.

A year ago we were told that Bessie's vision was about 85 percent in daylight and 50 percent in dim light. Now she perceives about 50 percent of her world in the sun and more like 10 percent when it's dark. I've developed my own way of testing Bessie's vision: the batted-ball method. Just as in the old days I take Bessie out on the field next to our house. She somehow senses that a bat and ball are involved because she prances like a show horse in anticipation. I throw the ball up, start to swing and off Bessie goes in pursuit. She runs thirty yards at full speed before she stops to get her bearings. Bessie is so excited at the prospect of finding the ball that she neglects to verify it's been hit.

When she returns I roll the ball to her and she picks it up in her mouth. Once it has her scent the ball becomes a beacon, sending out an invisible beam that her heightened sense of smell can zero in on. I hit the ball and Bessie takes off like a hound after a fox.

Sometimes it takes her a few minutes to track down the ball, but she *always* finds it. The trouble now is that when she locates the ball and turns around with it in her mouth, she can't see *me*. The poor thing has found her trophy, but she is a retriever and finding the prize is only half the process. She knows I'm out there somewhere, so her nose goes up in the air like a periscope, her ears perk up like antennae and she searches.

There is a fearlessness in Bessie's spirit. She refuses to give up the game she loves, no matter how difficult or puzzling it becomes. A lot of instinct is at work here, but ample doses of courage, resilience and defiance are also in play. Bessie and I are performing a delicate balancing act. At what point does this game become a mockery of a great dog's fading glory? At what point does it become more comical than productive, more cruel than pleasant?

I take my cue from Bessie. Somehow, this wonderful girl can still speak with her eyes. Based on my voice, she knows where to find me and returns the ball to my feet. She looks at me with a penetrating, haunting stare. And though I know she cannot really see me, her message is clear: "Don't you dare stop hitting balls for me, ever, no matter how hopeless I may seem."

Bessie reminds me that we are defined more by our spirit and effort than by our results. Resilience is the inevitable trump card that allows us to keep playing long after our skill and youth have simmered and boiled off. I imagine myself, a very old man, taking fifteen minutes to walk just a hundred yards, shuffling along at a snail's pace, refusing to sit still despite logical reasons that support a sedentary lifestyle. Instead, I'll emulate my hero, Bessie. And if people want to laugh at me, so what? Like Bessie, I won't know or care.

CHAPTER 20

Ice Hockey

Life is either a daring adventure or nothing at all.
—Helen Keller

F all passes and another winter arrives without a lot of fanfare. Halloween, Thanksgiving and Christmas come and go with apparently thoughtful adjustments from Bessie so that each of these special occasions simultaneously sustains and loses some of its luster. Our girl knows what to do, sort of, but has trouble executing some of the details. Through it all Bessie retains a relentless hunger for the act of retrieving. So when the lake in New Hampshire freezes over I grab my skates, my hockey stick and a puck to see if we might find a new activity for our increasingly blind dog. It is time to teach Bessie to play ice hockey.

The lesson begins in our kitchen with the introduction of the hockey puck as a potential toy. Like a kid in Canada Bessie seems to have an instinct for the game, understanding that possession of the puck is the key to success. As we head to the lake I think Bessie expects to go swimming. When we get there the slippery ice is a mystery until the skates are laced up and Bessie hears more than watches me glide away from her with the puck on my stick. A light goes on in her primal brain and somehow she intuitively comprehends that a new game is underway.

The surface of the ice is white and the puck is black, a contrast that works in Bessie's favor. I skate around the lake and she uses her toenails to dig into the frozen surface to keep up. Once she is acclimated we slide to a stop. Bessie senses what we are about to do and when the puck is slapped she scampers off in pursuit of this sliding black rubber disc, following her best guess as to where it will end up. As long as the puck makes noise skittering across the ice Bessie is able to track it, like a greyhound chasing a make-believe rabbit. When she has the puck in her mouth its texture must trigger some impulse deep in her DNA. She squeezes it in a vice grip as if it's the last frozen cookie on Earth. Only the familiar command, "Drop," puts the puck back in play.

Keep in mind that the temperature is about five degrees Fahrenheit and the wind chill makes it feel like ten below. So what? Bessie is in her element and at some level in her Labrador retriever brain she is meeting expectations, bringing home the bird and dropping it at my feet. Nothing else matters. Nothing!

The only problem is when the puck slides beyond where her instinct tells her it might be. Then, Bessie is befuddled—clueless, really. It's as if she's aged on the run. When the puck leaves the hockey stick Bessie acts like an eager, carefree puppy. As it slides farther away from her she becomes a lost, confused old lady, barely remembering what she is looking for. Here is a lifetime transpiring in a matter of seconds. Whenever she loses the puck I help her find it and her enthusiasm and youth return with no memory of the foggy period.

My takeaway—watching this fearless, handicapped good girl going for it with all of her heart—is simple. I can make decisions based on what the worst possible outcome may be, or I can emulate Bessie and live on the adrenalin that comes with going for it despite the risk of failure. I know that Bessie, looking at me with those dark, hopeful, increasingly sightless eyes, will never understand a cautious approach. After all, she is a hockey player now, and we all know how tough and resilient hockey players are.

CHAPTER 21

Instincts Take Over

Trust instinct to the end, even though you can give no reason.—Ralph Waldo Emerson

Eventually the snow melts and spring arrives with all of its promise for new beginnings. For Bessie that means daily baseball practice on the field next to our house. The boys on the team love Bessie and admire the way she still runs down batted balls, or tries to, even though she has trouble seeing them. As the spring term ends and the traditions of the school year pass one by one, Ashley and I are once again wondering what the summer will bring. We are curious how Bessie will handle it when her toy is tossed in the lake for the first time, what boat rides will be like and if she'll still enjoy paddleboarding around the lake.

Our reservations vanish the first day back when, as if lifting the lid of a treasure chest, we open the cottage's squeaky screen door and resume summer patterns. Ashley and I are pretending that nothing has really changed, but of course Bessie is a different dog now, or so we think. Nonsense! The first time we toss her toy in the water she bounds after it as usual. It takes her longer to find it, but once she tracks it down her teeth clamp onto the orange cylinder and she brings it back like the wounded bird her brain tells her it is. Bessie's instincts and memory are taking over and it's beautiful to watch.

Later that first day back we put our Boston Whaler in the water. Sunset cruises are a tradition on the lake and one of Bessie's favorite activities. In the past she would be the first one in the boat, hopping off the dock without encouragement to take her customary place on the bow while waiting for the humans.

This time Ashley and I get into the boat and there is Bessie standing on the dock, feeling or smelling what should happen in a general sense, but needing some clarification. Ashley slaps the deck of the boat and says encouragingly, "It's okay, come on Bess." Somewhere deep in Bessie's brain her memory takes over and she jumps over the foot-high railing into the boat. Imagine a person doing the same thing blindfolded. Impossible. But Bessie jumps without hesitation and with a straight face, expecting no praise or approval. "I'm in the boat; let's go," her body language implies. Amazing! Forty minutes later Bessie disembarks with the same humble nonchalance.

The last test comes the next morning when I bring the paddleboard down to the water's edge. I tap the top of the board and splash a little water so Bessie can get her bearings. As she stands on the dock I slide the nose of the paddleboard under the dock's edge, tap the surface of the board again, give her a little encouragement, and Bessie steps aboard. With perfect balance she gently works her way to the nose, sits down and off we go. Imagine trying this yourself, in the dark.

We paddle around the lake with unseen people calling to Bessie, welcoming her to summer. She acts as if she can see them. Like a queen in a parade Bessie graciously acknowledges their greetings with vague awareness by slowly wagging her tail, appearing to be arrogant when all she is, really, is blind. And on we paddle, me crying inside with a strange mix of sadness, joy and pride, and The Queen blissfully enjoying the sounds and smells, but not the sights. As we pass a friend who knows of Bessie's condition he says, "She is lucky to have you." "You're wrong," I reply. "It's the other way around. We are lucky to have her."

CHAPTER 22

Barking at the Dark

You've got to be very careful if you don't know where you are going, because you might not get there.
—Yogi Berra

S elf-worth is important. Deep down we all need to know that we are essential to the well-being of others, that our lives have purpose. This is on my mind because after forty-two years at our boarding school Ashley and I are retiring. It's six months away so we have time to wrap our minds around it and consider what will come next. After a lifetime of taking care of other people's children and living in an intense, intimate, supportive community, life will be different. This change won't sneak up on us the way Bessie's blindness has been slowly stalking her. While can anticipate the changes and plan for them, her fading sight has the potential to end her career prematurely with no chance for preparation.

As a Labrador retriever and the caretaker of our family, Bessie draws her self-worth from fetching thrown items and protecting us from perceived intruders. That's her purpose in life, along with eating any tasty tidbits she can get down her throat. When she could see clearly Bessie would size up a car pulling into the driveway, watch the squirrels outside the window, check the birds on the feeder or the animals in the backyard and decipher friend from foe before deciding to bark.

One time the school's baseball team was warming up before a game on the field next to our house. Bessie walked among the boys collecting pats on the head and ear scratches. When the opposing team's bus arrived Bessie barked like a warrior at the players as they disembarked. Some of the more cautious ones were so afraid they stayed on the bus. It was great! And when the occasional deer, coyote or fox wandered into our backyard Bessie shifted into full-on attack mode, confident as the clear-eyed guardian of her family.

It's different now. Even with her heightened senses of smell, hearing and self-awareness, Bessie is handicapped in her role as watchdog. So to sustain her self-worth Bessie barks more often now. We call it "barking at the dark." Day or night, she will come and find us and begin barking. We look out the windows...nothing. No intruders outside, no strange cars in the driveway, no animals in the yard. Yet if you watch Bessie you'd think a troupe of axe murderers is storming the house. On Bessie's face, even with those cloudy, foggy eyes, there is a look of terror and she is compelled to share her fear for our safety. The only thing is, I think she's faking it to get attention.

When this happens we indulge Bessie. We take her outside and let her bark at the dark until she feels we are safe again. Then we pat her on the back and go inside, her dignity intact. We are pretty sure Bessie is making up these fake invasions because she never interrupts her meals to bark, no matter what, and once she goes to sleep at about ten-thirty, Bessie is quiet as a mouse until we let her out in the morning. But if we ignore her for too long during the day, or if she feels irrelevant, Bessie becomes a security guard keeping away the bad guys, even if they are not really there.

Feeling irrelevant is becoming a bigger and bigger issue for Bessie. When we go on walks and encounter other dogs she has no idea whether she is rubbing noses with a Chihuahua or a German shepherd. There is no body language to read, just smell, touch and sound. She has always been the antithesis of an alpha dog, a doormat, really. But now Bessie gets a look of utter panic on her face during canine encounters. She can't tell if we are under attack or at a party and this uncertainty freaks her out. "Tell me what to do," she seems to be saying, "and fast, before I make a huge mistake." After I say, "It's okay, Bess," a couple of times, she regains her composure and poise.

Reading sign is the skill of sizing up a situation and knowing your responsibilities. Bessie can no longer read sign. The hardest part is that she appears to be stupid now, walking into things and staring into space, but of course she is not. She is brilliant, coping courageously with a world that is more challenging each day. We shower her with praise and encouragement to sustain her spirit. So far, so good—her confidence is intact.

With retirement on the horizon I'll probably be going through the same transition as Bessie, working to stay relevant and feel needed. I wonder what my version of barking at the dark will be and if my friends and family will go along with it?

CHAPTER 23

Catching a Buzz

Joy, temperance, and repose, slam the door on the doctor's nose.—Henry Wadsworth Longfellow

Most days I am the first one downstairs in the morning. Sometimes I sneak around quietly like a commando, tiptoe to the mudroom where Bessie sleeps and stealthily open the door. No matter how silent I try to be, Bessie is always on her feet, nose to the door and looking up with empty eyes that are somehow still filled with expectation. Her rapidly advancing blindness doesn't seem to be eroding her spirit or enthusiasm and her positive energy is uplifting, like strong coffee on New Year's morning. She behaves as if she believes each day that her vision will return as soon as she steps into the backyard.

Sadly, Bessie confirms her blindness each morning when she walks into something, like a planter or porch furniture, but she deals with it as a mere inconvenience and heads enthusiastically into the day. The same is true when we let her out in the afternoon or evening. There is a level of energy in Bessie now that we have trouble understanding. She can't *wait* to get out into the apple orchard that grows beyond the perennial garden behind our house.

My initial belief was that the open space of the orchard empowered a feeling of independence in Bessie; that she somehow remembered there was lots of open space back there among the scattered apple trees. I was wrong. Bessie is attracted to the orchard for the alcohol. This cagey, wily, six-year-old Lab has figured out that the apples lying on the ground are filled with fermented apple cider. Like an alcoholic on the sly, Bessie slowly and casually saunters into the orchard and then devours the nectar-filled fruit. It may be my imagination, but I swear Bessie is catching a buzz before breakfast...and then again in the afternoon, and definitely before dinner. She is self-medicating her grief about going blind.

I can't say I ever saw Bessie stagger or behave inappropriately, but she sure seemed happier and less concerned during the fall. Eventually the apples rotted and disappeared into the ground or under the snow and Bessie got her drinking problem under control. She is selective in her choice of poison; I sometimes hold a glass of wine in her direction and she turns away, so I guess we only have to worry during apple season. What a piece of work this dog is.

CHAPTER 24

She's Upstairs Again

I kind of quit surfing when I got out of high school, but then a few years ago I started to take it up again. I'm not an expert by any means, but it's so wonderful to get out in the ocean and get a different perspective on things.—Jeff Bridges

I am sitting in the bathtub one evening around ten unwinding from a rewarding day. Suddenly Bessie walks into the bathroom and lies down beside the tub as if it is the most normal thing in the world. This is significant because Bessie has not been upstairs in our house for almost three years. The stairs have become a treacherous, unpredictable obstacle course. Each time I head upstairs Bessie looks in my direction with a forlorn expression of exclusion. I feel like I am abandoning her, entering a private club she cannot join. In her mind "upstairs" has become some mysterious place humans retreat to. And when I descend the stairs she always seems to be waiting for me.

So you can imagine my surprise when Bessie walks in the bathroom and plops down next to the tub for a nap. Her body language implies that I should not make a big thing out of this, so I don't. I know she must have a reason, but for now it's just good to know our blind dog has conquered her fears. The reason for Bessie's adventure and her corresponding courage soon become evident. Soap! She loves the stuff and must have smelled it from the kitchen. And when Bessie smells a snack no obstacle will stand in her way. Sure enough, as soon as I lather up she awakens and begins licking the soap off me as if it's ice cream.

When the bath is over and she's had her fill, I watch Bessie descend the stairs. She is like a robot, mechanically counting the steps: one, two, three, four, five, six—pause on the landing—one, two, three, four, five, six—back on the first floor again. The sequence must have been resting there in her memory all these years like a dance routine. I watch her go up the stairs the same way, summoning her confidence with a couple of false starts, and then off she goes: one, two, three, four, five, six—pause on the landing—one, two, three, four, five, six—arrive at the destination. Miraculous! All for the sweet taste of soap.

Gradually, Bessie's comfort with going upstairs expands and we find her there when we return to the house after work or a night out. Freedom, a sense of mischief, independence, who knows? But Bessie is expanding her world at the same time it's shrinking exponentially. What a trooper.

Aging can make cowards of the bravest people. From somewhere in her heart and brain this blind dog summons the courage to head into the unknown. There has to be a terrifying aspect to this for Bessie, mixed with anticipation and intoxicating freedom. What is the source of her bravery? How does she know the last step is not off a ledge to a place unknown, down some deep hole? Maybe she doesn't. But she takes the step anyway, inspiring me again with her quiet confidence and sense of adventure which keep her young at heart long after there is any logical reason for behaving that way. It's a matter of will. My ambition is to follow Bessie's example in the years ahead.

CHAPTER 25

Right-Eyed Bessie

There are some people who see a great deal and some who see very little in the same things.
—Thomas Henry Huxley

Bessie's left eye has clouded over now. It resembles a white, vintage marble. There is still minimal function in Bessie's right eye. Somehow, slivers of light still make it to her right retina, but inconsistently and unpredictably, like slow leaks in an old roof. When she is out in the backyard at night and I shine a flashlight to find her, only her right eye glows. The poor thing is like a car with a burned-out headlight, though no bulb can replace it.

It won't be long before both lights are out. In the meantime, she remains a bright-faced girl hoping for action. Bessie's blindness has come on so gradually, in such tiny increments, that she probably can't remember when her world was full of light and objects had clear definition. She modifies her lifestyle without really knowing she is doing it, like a person living in a foreign country who one day realizes he has learned to speak a new language naturally, without instruction.

I sometimes wish I had filmed Bessie's transition to blindness. Her mannerisms are pretty much unchanged. Her body remembers what to do, but the graceful girl is now awkward at times. She is like a ballet dancer who never had to think about her movements in relation to space, gradually becoming clumsy. All of the walls and furniture she bumps into now are Bessie's tutors, mere annoyances.

Throughout her transition to sightlessness we have not coddled Bessie, deciding it is better to let her figure things out. She is holding on to old ways and still charging ahead like a reckless teenager getting out of school in the afternoon, but we are beginning to see a hint of uncharacteristic caution seeping in reluctantly.

Bessie's fate is most clearly evident when she feels she is alone. With no sound for guidance her world in solitude is empty, confusing and perhaps a bit frightening. At these times her facial expression is hollow and lifeless. I've seen that same look on people in nursing homes and I don't ever want to wear that expression. If that day comes hopefully I'll have the spirit Bessie exhibits hiding behind her mask.

When you call Bessie by name she snaps her head in your direction, but her gaze is off just a bit. She looks over your shoulder or to the side of you with an expression that says, "Is that you? Are you there?" It's inspiring to see Bessie's expression change from empty to full in a flash when she hears a familiar voice. Her world has four and one-tenth dimensions now —sound, taste, touch, smell and just a tiny bit of sight in that right eye.

In the sound dimension every decibel is vivid; each vibration paints a clear picture in Bessie's mind. Her refined sense of taste instructs her whether to chew and swallow something or spit it out. Bessie's sense of touch turns her into a bumper car, bouncing off objects in her way, and her smell dimension is intense. If you drop a peanut on the floor she will set her bearings on the sound and her nose will find it, guaranteed. But in the sight dimension there's just a pinhole left in her right eye, and it's closing fast. There is very little sunlight in Bessie's life beyond what she feels on her fur. The sun shines outward from her heart now.

In some ways our six-and-a-half-year-old is in her prime. If you watch Bessie from a distance in an open field you will see a dog in full. The closer you get, the clearer her handicap. And when you get close enough to pat her, Bessie will flinch at the touch, just for an instant, until she knows she is safe. That is when you realize she can't see. And of course those empty eyes that are turning white tell the story.

I see and sense the world differently now. Moments of natural beauty are clearer, richer, more brilliant. Faces are portraits, each one a memorized masterpiece. Shadows are mysterious, fleeting, treasured images painted by the sun. I want to be sure that if the lights go out for me someday I'll have a catalogue of images in my memory bank, just as Bessie does.

In the meantime, we will continue to sit in the sun together and *feel* the world around us. If Bessie senses I'm next to her she'll nudge me to scratch her ears, ears that are as soft as the oldest T-shirt in your dresser. And she'll sigh just like she did when she could see clearly, because with her eyes closed she still can.

CHAPTER 26

Cotton Balls

When life's got you down, keep your head up... you can't see the ground anyway.—Nicole Rae

We often speculate whether Bessie can see anything at all and wonder if perhaps tiny fragments of light are somehow still getting through and stimulating her optic nerve. That question is settled a few days after her seventh birthday when Bessie goes for her annual checkup. It's like being with a movie star when we enter the doctor's office. The staff stops what they are doing and gathers around to admire Bess and take note of her condition.

Her untreatable blindness is something we've all watched progress in slow motion, and as her vision diminished Bessie's celebrity increased. All of this occurred with utter indifference by Bessie. Any sympathy directed her way has been ignored because for her this slow fade into darkness was not inflicted through malice or intention. It's the way her life naturally unfolded and she accepts it with her tail wagging. That's why the people in the vet's office are so enamored of her. Call it dignity or cluelessness, but there is absolutely no sorrow or regret in Bessie and even the most jaded person has to admire that.

We've been wondering what the final test for blindness will be, what device the doctor might roll out to make a conclusive diagnosis. Ashley and I are pretty sure Bessie's lights have gone out for good, but there is nothing scientific about our analysis—it's just a sense we have. Expecting to see Bessie fitted in some complicated, high-tech device that allows us to peer into those two milky white holes on her sweet face, we are relieved to see the doctor walk in with a handful of cotton balls. Bessie must overhear us because her ears perk up. If there is a ball involved she knows there is fun ahead. Not in this case, though.

How ironic that the ultimate test for determining Bessie's utter blindness involves an element of her favorite activity. The vet stands about five feet away and, one by one, tosses half a dozen cotton balls at her face from different angles. She doesn't blink or flinch, not at all. She accepts each one like a tough boxer on the ropes with his hands down, taking punches in the late rounds. The little pieces of fluff bounce off her nose, eyes and forehead silently and painlessly, but in my mind each one lands on the floor with a loud crash. The long, slow fade is over. What originally was supposed to take just twelve months has in fact stretched over two and a half years.

The tears well up in our eyes as the finality of the journey sinks in. But there are no tears from Bessie. She is sitting on the examination table with her eyes wide open and ears at attention, sensing that someone is throwing mysterious things at her. She remembers that in the past there was a treat at the end of each doctor appointment, and her instincts tell her this visit is winding down. She is even drooling a bit in happy expectation of the cookies that are coming.

When something winds down for Bessie that only means something else is winding up. When we get home she jumps out of the car and begins dancing in circles when Ashley promises her a walk. And off they go with Bessie leading the way, guided by a memory burned into the joyful place in her brain where walks are stored. Yes, off they go, across the baseball field and onto a path in the woods that Bessie has been walking for seven years. No leash, just a keen sense of where to go based on experience and instinct wrapped up in scents and sounds that keep her on the trail. She is connected to Ashley by some invisible tether of trust.

Heaven forbid Bessie stop for a minute doing the things she loves just because of a little complication. I watch her disappear on her walk, embarrassed that I ever complained about *anything* and vowing to never do it again, ever.

CHAPTER 27

A Retriever Forever

Being fearless isn't being 100 percent not fearful, it's being terrified but you jump anyway.—Taylor Swift

O ne of the front teeth on Bessie's lower jaw is chipped in half. There are little scars and nicks all over the end of her nose and around her eyes. These are the trophies of a chocolate Lab who was born to bring thrown, kicked or batted objects back to the person who launched them.

If you think Bessie would let a little thing like blindness interfere with this deep-rooted instinct, think again. Let me add that I am not a mean, thoughtless owner. On the contrary, denying her this pleasure would be the real cruelty. The acquired wounds and injuries are her medals, earned in relentless pursuit of happiness. Bessie would be heartbroken if we stopped the retrieving games just to keep her safe. She would never understand, never.

One time she took off at full speed after a tossed ball, but in the wrong direction. Before I could stop her she ran straight into a tree. Momentarily stunned, with blood dripping out of both nostrils, Bessie would not be consoled. She squirmed away from my sympathetic embrace and took off with her bleeding nose to the ground, eventually finding the ball, retrieving it and dropping it at my feet. As she stood there with her tail wagging, her watering, blind eyes wide open and her body trembling with expectation, I had no other option but to throw the ball again. Which I did, and which I will continue to do every day until my arm falls off or Bessie dies. She will never forgive me otherwise.

When we are at the lake now, Bessie's retriever instincts are even more compelling. She jumps in, intuitively knows where deeper water is and swims away from shore. We fling her water toy into the air and when it splashes on the surface Bessie changes course and swims in that direction, eventually finding the toy with her nose. Like a homing pigeon she senses where the shore is and, aided by our cheers and clapping hands, brings her prize back. When her feet touch land Bessie proudly drops the toy, plunges back into the water and the game continues. Sometimes she swims into the dock, or bumps into our small boat, but these are just subtle messages she reads by Braille with her happy face.

One day I come around the corner of our tiny cottage and find Bessie with her front feet up on a small table. I tiptoe back behind the corner so as not to be sensed by her magical awareness. From my secret vantage point I witness an astounding scene unfolding. With her acute sense of smell Bessie has located her favorite toy on this three-foot-high table and is finding a way to move it within reach of her eager mouth. Mission accomplished, she sets out to find me so we can play. I make some noise and moments later there she is, imploring me to throw the toy in the lake. I have no choice. Off we go.

Bessie refuses to back off. I sometimes wonder if she is stubborn, courageous or just living blissfully in denial. But upon further reflection, who cares? She is full of joy, endlessly living in anticipation of the next adventure and willing to get banged around a bit in the process. What would the alternative be, living her life on a leash or tied to a chain so as not to bloody her nose or chip a tooth now and then? Bessie would *never* forgive me for choosing the safe route, cheating her out of a full life through my own caution. No thanks. Not for Bessie, and not for me. Chipped teeth, bloody noses and a few scars are nothing compared to the unmet potential of a life spent looking out the window as a safe spectator. I'll take Bessie's example for a model of how to *live*.

CHAPTER 28

Talking to Dogs

It's no coincidence that man's best friend cannot talk.—Anonymous

I f you are or have ever been a dog owner you have an alternate voice that comes from some tender back corner of your brain. We'll call it your *dog voice*. It's a voice you keep private for the most part because to go public with its tone, inflection and vocabulary could ruin your reputation and career. But all dog lovers have this special voice, ready to be called into action at a moment's notice.

Sometimes, when watching particularly gruff, arrogant or aggressive people in action, I wonder what their dog voices sound like. What is President Donald Trump's dog voice, or LeBron James's or Megyn Kelly's? How about Hillary Clinton's dog voice? Maybe along with releasing tax returns, candidates for elected office should submit secretly recorded copies of their dog voices as a qualification. It might be interesting.

When your pet can't see the vocabulary of your dog voice expands exponentially. I sometimes look over my shoulder before talking to Bessie because if someone overheard our conversation they might lock me up. You see, when your dog is blind you begin to think you have to interpret the world for her. Perhaps more alarming is that you begin to believe that your dog can't function without you, which is utter nonsense.

There are a number of dog voices I use with Bessie. One of them is the *Be Careful* voice when it's necessary to alert her that the terrain is changing or that something is in her path. Then there is the *End of the Day Snuggle* voice which is the most private of all. I'd pay a healthy ransom to prevent a recording of me talking to Bessie in this context from becoming public.

Sometimes when Bessie is meeting new people we withhold the fact that she is blind. In each case, when her handicap is discovered people change their dog voices, adding a more sympathetic tone. We discourage this because we believe Bessie works the angle to get food.

Our dear friends Kevin and Diane sometimes watch Bessie for us when we travel. Bessie absolutely loves these people, partly because they have such wonderful dog voices. When Bessie hears Diane's velvety voice ask, "Are you coming to stay with Auntie?" she is overcome with joy and will abandon us without looking back.

Kevin lets Bessie help him with yard work. A neighbor listening to Kevin's ongoing dialogue was shocked to discover he was talking to a dog rather than a person. Kevin's intellect and sense of humor are as sharp as a knife's edge and Bessie seems to enjoy the enlightening aspect of his conversations with her, especially when blended with Diane's affectionate voice, which Bessie laps up like warm butter.

We all need to be more in touch with our dog voices. When interviewing teaching candidates I used to pay particular attention if a dog wandered into the picture, listening closely to the tone and melody of the candidate's dog voice. It provided an unfiltered look into the most empathetic and nurturing aspects of the person's soul. Marriage proposals should be delayed until thoroughly vetting a future spouse's dog voice. The same goes for college admission, getting a driver's license or agreeing to sit next to someone on a long airplane flight. Just think how much less pretentious we would all be if our dog voices were part of our profiles.

A final thought: what is it like when someone speaks to *you* in their dog voice? May we all live long enough to find out.

CHAPTER 29

Angel's Halo

Courage is the most important of all the virtues because without courage, you can't practice any other virtue consistently.—Maya Angelou

S ome recent houseguests from Los Angeles fell in love with Bessie. Claire, the humble, stylish, stiff-upper-lip Englishwoman with a giant heart joined the swashbuckling, romantic, sharp-witted twins Salvator and Emmanuel for a weekend visit. Spending time with these people is like being featured in a well-directed Hollywood movie where even the smallest event can become a memorable scene. Sounds, colors and *life* become more vivid in their company. This trio could make a fortune renting themselves out for entertainment. When these friends departed our house felt empty, like a dance hall the morning after a party.

Salvator and Emmanuel chattered away like chipmunks, providing a rich, humorous commentary on *everything*. But it was quiet, reflective, observant Claire who could bring things sharply into focus with just a few well-chosen words. As the trio's visit stretched into the second day it became clear that Bessie and Claire were bonding. Maybe Bessie's ancestors are from England, because with all of these characters to choose from, Bessie always seemed to sit near Claire. They connected, deeply.

A couple of weeks after our charming guests departed a package arrives in the mail, addressed to Bessie. It is from Claire. Included with her sweet, heartfelt thank-you note is a well-designed garment for blind dogs called Muffin's Halo. Claire's thoughtful intention is to provide some much needed protection for Bessie's increasingly scarred face. The halo has a bar made of a space-age composite material that guards a blind dog from head injury, like the simple protection on football helmets in the early 1960s. Google a picture of Lance Alworth and you'll see what I mean.

Here's how the halo works: Bessie is snugly fitted with a sleeveless vest that attaches under her chest. The face mask bar is then fastened to the vest by Velcro and bends out in a semicircle around her nose. When we first outfit Bessie I think we hurt her feelings a little bit because we are laughing so hard. Really, here is this rugged chocolate Lab in a red vest with a bar protruding about three inches from her nose. Remember that Bessie can't see this apparatus; she can only sense it. In her typical trusting way off she goes, poking around the house and the surrounding area, clueless as to how she looks, but vaguely aware that something is different.

The thing is, it *works*! Whoever designed this device really understands blind dogs. Bessie explores the yard with it on, sniffs along the shore of the lake, falls asleep in the sun and basically acts normally. Occasionally we hear her bang into furniture, the side of the house, cars in the driveway or the metal table on our porch, but it's the face bar taking the brunt of the impact, not her nose or teeth, so we let her try it for a few days.

One day I see the halo hanging mysteriously off the gearshift of our lawn tractor. Bessie is nowhere in sight. Upon closer examination I notice the sturdy face bar is bent out of shape. When I locate Bessie she is sound asleep in the sun on the hill behind our house, wearing her vest. Apparently the face bar got hooked on the gearshift and she somehow wrenched herself free, proving to be stronger than the heavy-duty Velcro that is supposed to secure the bar. We bend it back into place and reattach it with little trouble. Life goes on.

What left a mark with me was the fact that I never heard a bark or a yelp from Bessie when she got entangled with the tractor. Imagine the sense of panic she must have felt when suddenly her mobility was impeded by an unseen attacker. *I can't see this captor, and I can't get away from it,* she must have thought to herself. Yet, in her typical stoic, courageous fashion Bessie somehow found a way to free herself, and it clearly wasn't easy.

It is a sign of strength to ask for help. I understand that. Yet asking for help with everything, or always expecting others to get you out of a jam denies you the opportunity to be resourceful and self-reliant, which contributes to self-worth. Staying young at heart and solving your own problems as you get older is not always a natural instinct. It takes considerable effort and determination—the kind Bessie has.

Claire lovingly sent the halo to make Bessie's life easier and less painful. The halo also provides Bessie with a chance to prove her wonderful, independent spirit and determination with no one watching. And how we act when no one is watching reveals the truest picture of our character. Bessie aces this test. She may have lost her halo, but she is still our angel.

CHAPTER 30

Love the One You're With

*I'm interested in the fact that the less secure a man is,
the more likely he is to have extreme prejudice.*
—Clint Eastwood

Bessie is not a particularly loyal animal. I know that in dog terms she loves Ashley and me most dearly and best of all, but she also loves everybody else she has ever encountered or will encounter in her life. When people come over for dinner they leave thinking they have somehow established a special bond with our old girl, a bond deeper than any other guest has been able to secure. The thing is, whether it's two or ten people, each leaves with that same feeling of personal attachment to Bessie.

One day Ashley and I neglect to let Bessie out of the car after taking her for a hike. We are in such a hurry to get ready for the dinner party we are hosting that we completely forget about her. When our friends arrive and Bessie is nowhere to be found, all twelve guests help search for her outside our house. One Bessie-lover goes deep into the woods calling her name. Each of these people has a connection with Bessie and is *worried.* Eventually she is located in the car and we all have a good laugh, but I marvel at the genuine level of concern Bessie generates in this diverse group of people. She just has that effect.

We now live full-time in rural New Hampshire and have a wonderful assortment of friends, delivery vans and contractors who pull into our driveway. Bessie greets every driver with her tail wagging and tries to climb into each vehicle. Should one of these visitors invite Bessie aboard and close the door, she would be fine sitting in the front seat, joyfully on her way to some adventure with a new pal. Regardless of their size, shape, gender, race, nationality, level of education or appearance, Bessie treats everyone she meets as a trusted partner; her welcome mat is always out. In the process she adds momentary value to people's lives and expects nothing in return. It's the way she lives.

When we travel Bessie stays with various nearby families. No matter whom we choose she wiggles, squirms and warbles with excitement as we pull in the driveway of her temporary caretakers. Some dogs get a little freaky when they are in new situations. Not Bessie. If there are people around she is in love with them, instantly. And it's not that she loves us less. She just has an endless supply of affection rooted in the fact that she cannot comprehend, conceive or even vaguely consider that whomever she's with is not kind and warmhearted. If Bessie encountered mean or callous behavior she would not be able to process it. She lacks those receptors. Cruelty would endlessly puzzle her.

One family that occasionally takes care of Bessie has two young children. It's like Christmas for this clan when we drop her off; the whole family receives her as a special gift. While we are away we receive pictures of Bessie dressed up in crazy costumes, Bessie on walks, Bessie in bed with the kids. She becomes part of their family, finding her place and settling in with a seamless ease.

Another family texted us a picture of Bessie enjoying a ride in a kayak. The other day she received an invitation in the mail to a three-year-old's birthday party. It's difficult for humans to assimilate to new situations with the natural ease Bessie demonstrates. She is like a gear that can fit into any engine and help it run better.

Offering unconditional, judgement-free acceptance of loved ones and complete strangers alike takes practice; it's not a natural tendency. We humans by and large are quick to pass judgement. People are smart or dull, attractive or unkempt, coordinated or clumsy. Country clubs and yacht clubs are notorious for passing judgement. If we are not careful we can fall into the trap of believing some of us are better or more important than others. That is not true.

For Bessie it's simple: As Crosby, Stills and Nash sang so many years ago, "Love the one you're with." To do that requires unlimited quantities of kindness and appreciation of differences. This can only happen if you empty the tanks of prejudice that hold you back from approaching life with an open mind and heart. I've learned this from Bessie, thank goodness, because it's nice having so many wonderful people around.

CHAPTER 31

Watching the Lights Go Out

Dying is a troublesome business: there is pain to be suffered, and it wrings one's heart; but death is a splendid thing—a warfare accomplished, a beginning all over again, a triumph. You can always see that in their faces.—George Bernard Shaw

Euthanizing a dog is at the same time a nightmare and a sweet dream filled with touching memories of a short life well lived, and as with most important things in life any attempt to minimize its impact is a mistake. People get bereavement leave for deaths in the family, but we are expected to lose our pets stoically, or on weekends. This doesn't make sense when you are in the middle of such a passing.

When parents pass away there is profound sorrow, but often parents and their adult children are separated by life experiences and distance. It's sad and deeply painful, of course, but there is a natural rhythm to these transitions. When pets die, and certainly in our case dogs, it's a different deal. Ashley and I have sent four off so far.

Bessie's predecessor, Bow, was also a chocolate Lab. Before Bessie he was the best dog we'd ever owned. When Bow, a cancer survivor, was ready to call it quits at eleven years old he walked calmly and with dignity into our front yard in subzero temperatures and lay down in the snow. Nothing could revive his spirit, not even cookies, which in his prime could be used to get Bow to do *anything.* He had made up his mind that he was done.

When we took him to the vet I just knew that Bow understood what came next. Holding his face softly in my hands, I looked in his beautiful brown eyes and spoke gently to him as the doctor administered the lethal, painless injection. Suddenly, the lights in his eyes went out. Just like that. It was as if a switch had been thrown. Bow was gone.

I was comforted in a weird way by the fact that when old Bow left this world the face and voice of someone who loved him were his last earthly memories before the journey to doggie heaven, or wherever. He did not travel alone. The experience is as vivid today as it was all those years ago and I am glad to have made his death so intimate and personal. You only get one chance at these things, you know. I was at my mother's bedside for her final, rattling breath and I'm glad.

What will it be like for Bessie? She is eight now and in her prime. It's way too early for a deathwatch, but in a way we have watched a part of her die for almost four years. What will it be like when her hearing starts to go and, God forbid, her sense of smell? What about arthritis? Labs are famous for their arthritis. The hardest thing to imagine is Bessie limping and struggling to retrieve her ball when she can no longer hear it drop or smell it. I shake my head just thinking about it because she is so damn resilient that I know she will somehow figure out a solution...until that day.

Until that day when Bessie sends us a signal that she's ready to fold her tent. Until that day when she is tired of running into things and searching for balls and toys that are finally just too hard to track down. Until that day when carrying the extra stress and strain, multiplied by her handicaps, is too much for her. Until that day when she is exhausted from watching out for us and shouldering a spirit that is finally so heavy it weighs her down and those strong, steady legs buckle.

Before Bessie departs our world I will hold her face in my hands, look straight into her sightless eyes and talk to her in my most intimate dog voice. I will tell her what a blessing she has been for us, how much value she's added to our lives and how lucky we are that she picked us to take her home all those years ago. And then, I know that even in those white, empty eyes somehow I'll see her lights go out. There is just too much life in this girl to imagine otherwise.

This story, though it ends in speculation about Bessie's death, is fully and enthusiastically about *living life*. Bessie unknowingly floods me with daily reminders that each of us alone is in charge of our spirit and outlook. We can think of ourselves as poor, weak victims of unlucky turns, or the happy celebrants and survivors of life's endless challenges and tests. Our girl is my hero, plain and simple. I have been inspired by her enormous strength and embarrassed by my comparative, lame weakness.

As I write these final lines Bessie is snoring on her bed, resting up for tomorrow which will soon be another new, best day for her. When my body and mind tell me it's time to let go, I hope someone I love will hold my face in their hands, look into my eyes and speak soothingly. It's selfish, of course, but for a fleeting moment I might have a glimpse of what Bessie will know when her lights go out for good. Not a bad way to leave the dance floor, don't you think?

Postscript

How wonderful it is that nobody need wait a single moment before starting to improve the world.—Anne Frank

There is a permanent wrinkle in the middle of Bessie's forehead, the result of opening her eyes as wide as she absolutely can for most of her waking hours. Try it for just a minute; it's exhausting. A human in Bessie's situation would have resigned herself to the finality of her condition long ago, but not Bessie. She appears to believe her relentless effort will pay off and the world will somehow light up again if she just opens those white, filmy eyes wide enough. And if it doesn't, that's okay. Can you imagine having that kind of optimism? I can, because I live in its glow every day.

There are people who live courageously with profound handicaps and disabilities. Sometimes these are clearly visible, but often they are not. When you encounter these people talk with them, listen to them, smile with them, get cozy with their spirit and you will find a version of heaven on earth. Bessie taught me that.

According to the idea that every dog year is equal to about seven human years, when Bessie is halfway through her ninth year we will be roughly the same age. We are going to have a celebration that day, she and I, a big one.

Acknowledgements

This book would still be sitting on my laptop if not for the encouragement and enthusiasm offered by Jon Neuhaus. His relentless belief in the message of Bessie's Story was the fuel that turned a hobby into a book. Megan Reich George's gentle, firm guidance was invaluable in meeting deadlines and provided a partnership that blossomed into a friendship. Everyone should have a Megan in their life. Megan is also an expert photographer who captures the essence of her subjects. Nichole Enslin is a creative genius whose affection for Bessie resonates in the design elements of the book. Thanks to Martha Fairbairn and Mary Anne Greene for being among the first to validate the idea that Bessie's Story had value. And without the expert editing of Steven

Bauer and Jules Hucke, this book would be a clumsy attempt at good writing. The biggest thank you of all goes to my wife, Ashley. I knew each day she was going to ask, "Where are you with the book?" That was her way of saying she loved the story. Bessie, of course, was clueless throughout the process, bless her heart.

About the Author

Thomas W. Farmen is the Headmaster Emeritus of Rumsey Hall School in Washington, Connecticut. He and his wife Ashley worked in partnership at the school for over four decades and now live in rural New Hampshire. Dog owners for all of their forty-plus years of marriage, the Farmens travel, pursue a variety of outdoor interests and are active volunteers. Ashley is a New Hampshire Granite State Ambassador. Tom serves on the board for several non-profit organizations and is an ambassador at Mount Sunapee ski area. The Farmens have two adult sons.

CPSIA information can be obtained
at www.ICGtesting.com
Printed in the USA
FSHW012226090219
55555FS